The Dangers Of Ether As An Anesthetic

William Williams Keen

In the interest of creating a more extensive selection of rare historical book reprints, we have chosen to reproduce this title even though it may possibly have occasional imperfections such as missing and blurred pages, missing text, poor pictures, markings, dark backgrounds and other reproduction issues beyond our control. Because this work is culturally important, we have made it available as a part of our commitment to protecting, preserving and promoting the world's literature. Thank you for your understanding.

THE DANGERS OF ETHER AS AN ANESTHETIC

BY

W. W. KEEN, M.D., LL.D.

PHILADELPHIA

REPRINTED FROM
THE BOSTON MEDICAL AND SURGICAL JOURNAL
DECEMBER TWO
1915

THE DANGERS OF ETHER AS AN ANESTHETIC.*

By W. W. Keen, M.D., LL.D., Philadelphia.

Emeritus Professor of Surgery, Jefferson Medical College.

It is a great pleasure to tender my thanks to the Trustees and the Committee for their kind invitation to deliver an Ether Day Address.

In this historic place, 69 years ago this very day, occurred the first public use of ether as an anesthetic. We, who are accustomed to anesthesia, can hardly appreciate the courage of Warren and Morton on that memorable sixteenth of October, 1846. Surely also the bravery of the patient himself should not be overlooked. The name of Gilbert Abbott should always be held in remembrance.

I have often called the attention of my classes to a patient lying limp and apparently almost lifeless on the operating table. Lift the arm and it falls as if it were that of a corpse, touch the sensitive eye and the lids do not move. Cut the tender skin and it elicits no response. "Will he ever wake up?" "May not the flickering flame of life gradually fade away and forever?" "Have I not unwittingly killed this man?" Such must have been the insistent questions in the minds of those intrepid adventurers on that momentous occasion. How eagerly must they have welcomed the first faint evidences of returning consciousness! Had that young

* Address delivered at the Massachusetts General Hospital, on the sixty-ninth anniversary of Ether Day, October 16, 1915.

man died then and there, for how many years would the blessings of anesthesia have been withholden from the human race? Only eleven years earlier (1835) Père Velpeau, the great French surgeon, had said, "Eviter la douleur dans les opérations est un chimère qu'il n'est pas permis de poursuivre aujourd'hui." Who would have dared to repeat the dangerous experiment? For an experiment and a most hazardous experiment on a human being, it certainly was. Happily the result justified their temerity and millions have been blessed by the bravery of the surgeon, the anesthetist, and the patient.

In Berlin where I was a student in 1865-6 the story ran—and I believe it was authentic—that a short time earlier Henry B. Sands of New York, urging the greater safety of ether upon Langenbeck, at his request, gave ether for him in his clinic. The patient died on the table from the anesthetic. Naturally this deferred the use of ether in Germany for years and cost many lives.

In this city and this hospital my topic—The Dangers of Ether as an Anesthetic—may at the first blush seem ungracious. But our profession ever seeks the unvarnished and untarnished truth. To recognize that there *are* dangers is the first step in eliminating them. When life is at stake ignorance is not bliss. Forewarned is forearmed.

When I accepted the invitation and selected my topic, which had not been considered in any of the former Ether Day Addresses, I thought I had chosen an easy task. But I had hardly begun my work when I found that great progress had been made, as to much of which I was inadequately informed.

While I have had a large experience during a long and active surgical life, yet, in consequence of my retirement from active practice in 1907, I have had little or no personal experience with a number of the newest anesthetics and the latest modes of their administration. Accordingly, to make up for this lack, I devoted the past summer to the diligent study of the recent work on anesthetics and anesthesia by reading the extensive literature (especially the valuable physiological literature) of the last ten years, to a considerable correspondence (as the friends whom I persecuted will testify), and in the early autumn to some careful observations of the administration of anesthetics in Boston, New York, and Philadelphia. It has had all the fascination of novelty and the exhilaration of success.

When I began my medical studies in 1860 there were but two anesthetics in use, ether and chloroform. Now the many anesthetic drugs, the different methods of using them, by inhalation, by insufflation, by arterial or venous infusion, by different routes,—the mouth, the nose, the rectum, the colon—by local anesthesia, by spinal anesthesia, by one drug alone or by two or more, together, or in varying sequences, by simple or complicated apparatuses, or costly and elaborate chambers for differential pressure, have almost reached the classical "57 varieties."

During the last 10 years especially, the administration of anesthetics has been rapidly changing. It is becoming more and more an exact science instead of a mass of only empirical knowledge gained by practice and at the cost of danger or sometimes even of life. The multiplicity of valuable papers, the many set discussions in our medical societies, the exhaustive studies in our laboratories of research on the physics, the physiology and the chemistry of respiration and of anesthetics, the pathological changes observed in animals after intentional or accidental deaths, and after similar accidental deaths in human beings, the accumulated large statistics all demonstrate the deep interest, the scientific activity and the happy results of this new outburst of work in anesthesia.

One of the happiest results of this restless search for improvement is the rise of the *professional anesthetist*, an expert who by his mastery of the subject and his knowledge and prescience of danger, is able to avert or to remedy the danger—an expert who is more and more definitely coming to be recognized as comparable to the expert specialist in other departments of medicine and surgery. Says Bloodgood,[1] "Accumulated experience and reading . . . impress me more and more that anesthesia is an art in every sense of the word. *Specially trained anesthetists are necessary for safety.*"

The recent organization of the American Association of Anesthetists is another welcome evidence of progress. That professional specialists in anesthesia are greatly needed is strikingly shown by the frank reply to my questionnaire by the chief anesthetist of one of our best American hospitals. "To what do you attribute the deaths from ether?" was my question, and his reply began "Lack of skill in its administration."

That such experts are specially needed in America is shown by the fact that Gwathmey's American statistics[2] compared with those of Hewitt in England show that in this country our percentage of mortality from ether is *over three times as great as in Great Britain.*

Lest the general public who may read this may take alarm and exaggerate the dangers of ether, let me say at once that the deaths are estimated in various statistics as being only one death in 4533 administrations in America (Gwathmey), one in 5112 in Germany,[3] one in 16,302 in Great Britain,[4] and even only one in 50,000 (Rovsing).[5] But even if it be only one in 50,000 yet if that one is *your* boy, it is a sorry consolation to know that 49,999 others escaped.

As soon as I fixed upon my topic I sent out to the members of the American Surgical Association a questionnaire as to immediate and delayed ether deaths, requesting exact figures if they were available, and estimated figures if they were not. I received 67 replies, for which I tender my sincere thanks to my correspondents, a number of whom took much pains in compiling their statistics.

In 20 replies the figures were exact, though those of several active surgeons covered only a very few years. These returns showed,

Exact number of etherizations 262,002
Number of deaths 34
Or 1 death in 7,706 cases.

This is an improvement over Gwathmey's statistics, but the 34 deaths do not include some delayed deaths from pneumonia, nephritis, etc., which would probably bring the proportion down to about Gwathmey's figures or possibly worse. The 47 others—including, I regret to say, myself—could only estimate the number of their cases and deaths. The approximation to former statistics is gratifying as showing that the estimates were reasonably accurate and not too seriously optimistic.

Estimated number of etherizations 356,500
Estimated number of deaths 73

Or 1 death in 4,884 cases.

Both the estimated and the exact numbers show that we have still over three times the relative number of deaths as in Great Britain—a serious blot on our methods and results. This calls loudly for reform. The systematic use of duplicate charts, if collected from all available sources at intervals of five years, would show whether our results were improving or growing worse.

Compared with chloroform the dangers of ether are almost negligible. In Great Britain from 1910 to 1913 there were 700 inquests on deaths from anesthetics.* Of these, chloroform and its mixtures were responsible for 478 and ether for only 28. What is the relative *percentage* of fatalities of each, however, we do not know.

Personally I was brought up by the elder Gross in the Chloroform School, and I generally used it in my earlier cases. But I was soon convinced of my error, and for the last forty years I have used chloroform very, very rarely. I regard it either alone or in mixtures as a most dangerous anesthetic. With Bevan[7] and the Committee on Anesthesia of the American Medical Association,[8] I would urge that it should be discarded, excepting in a few special cases, also in the tropics and in military surgery on or near the battlefield, and on naval vessels during action.[9] In base hospitals and on hospital ships ether should be used.*

What we want is such an anesthetic and such anesthetists that there shall be *no deaths at all*. The search for this ideal anesthetic must be vigorously continued by experiment first upon ani-

* The papers and discussions on Anesthesia in the American Surgical Association in 1911 and 1915 will well repay perusal by every surgeon and every anesthetist.

mals. It has not yet been found, for every anesthetic known has its own dangers. I fear that even the best future anesthetic may not be wholly free from this possibility. As I have more than once pointed out, the ideal anesthetic should not preserve the consciousness of the patient, who would easily be terribly frightened at the least suspicion of danger, dangers which the surgeon has often encountered and easily vanquished. They would not only alarm the patient, but would often provoke uncontrollable physical movements which would cause serious dangers or entirely prevent the operation. This ideal anesthetic must also, if possible, be pleasant to administer, efficacious in abolishing all pain, free from noxious after-effects, and, if possible, without danger to life.

Our commonest anesthetic—ether—is to me, personally, both as surgeon and as patient, so little repulsive, and has such very slight danger in competent hands, that after having used it thousands of times with patients, and taken it myself on six different occasions, so far as any feeling of apprehension or repugnance is concerned, I would as lief lie down on the table and take ether as I would sit down at my table and eat my breakfast. No one, however, except by *force majeure* shall ever again give it to me as on the first occasion, in 1863, from a closed cone saturated with ether, which almost suffocated me. By the open drop method on a mask or the Allis inhaler,* which are practically equivalent, I have five other times been most pleasantly and efficaciously anesthetized. Not once have I had the least nau-

* The ether should be dropped on the Allis inhaler just as on a mask, slowly at first, faster and faster in a few minutes, but never poured in. Moderate rebreathing can be obtained by covering the upper surface by the hand.

sea. The long-continued ether taste and once some gas pains were the only unpleasant aftermaths. *Haud inexpertus loquor.*

"If patients could be educated to be as pleased when they are told that a surgical operation is necessary as they are when given a tonic, Utopia would be reached," says Bloodgood.

I reached such a Utopia some years ago when a young girl burst into tears upon my telling her that an operation for appendicitis was necessary. I tried to comfort her, but to my surprise she replied between her sobs that she was weeping for joy, for she had feared I would decide *not* to operate. Such Utopias, however, are not yet common, but I have found them gradually growing more frequent as the public are more and more convinced of the safety of modern operations and the danger of delay.

The students in our medical schools see a great many anesthetized patients, but their attention is given chiefly to the operation. Too often they receive little and in some schools no careful instruction in anesthesia. Far too frequently the function of the etherizer is delegated to the ever-changing junior residents, as if, forsooth, it were of minor importance. Next to the surgeon and even before his first operative assistant, in my opinion, stands the anesthetist, holding the scales of Life and Death. Happily, at least in the use of ether, the margin of safety is so wide that even inexperience and inattention are rarely harmful.

It should be the duty of our medical schools and their hospitals *to instruct all students in anesthesia and to give them experience* by having them administer anesthetics under the supervision of their experts. In view of the constant and necessary change of internes there should be on the staff of each division a permanent expert. In small hospitals at least one of the staff should make it his business to become an expert by constant study and practice.

The anesthetist should if possible always see the patient beforehand. He can thus establish an "*entente cordiale*" which will do much to prevent fear and other psychic elements of danger.

Gerster says that long ago he learned in Billroth's clinic to be careful with patients who exhibited fear but that he never understood the reasons until Crile and Yandell Henderson explained them.

The most striking instance of the *physical results of fear* I have ever known personally was a little girl of nine in my ward at the Jefferson Hospital. Her clothing had caught fire and she had been so dreadfully burned that a year after the accident I was compelled to amputate the left arm at the shoulder joint. She made an excellent recovery *per primam*, but had not been discharged because an old ulcer on the deltoid flap had not yet quite healed. Four weeks after the amputation she was suddenly awakened in the middle of the night by a nearby fire. The ward was high studded, the windows many. It was no wonder, therefore, that remembering her own dreadful experience and seeing the flames and the brightly illuminated ward, she should think the ward itself afire and become terrified. A thoughtful nurse took her temperature, which had long been normal, and found it 105.4°. The next morning it was 99°.

A similar but less striking instance is recorded by Crile and Lower[10] in which simple fear raised the temperature to 101.2° and the pulse to 150. Bloodgood[11] reports a case in which fear alone caused the blood pressure to fall in ten minutes from 140 to 80 m.m. In some cases even death has resulted from fear before an anesthetic has been given.

Crile is none too insistent upon the psychic as well as the physical conditions, which are so conducive to smooth recovery.

The *condition of the blood* should be ascertained beforehand in all serious operations, especially in anemic patients. DaCosta[12] and DaCosta and Kalteyer[13] and others have demonstrated the diminution of hemoglobin due to ether. While Mikulicz advised against any general anesthetic in case the hemoglobin was below 30%, DaCosta and Kalteyer represent a better present opinion by drawing the line at 50%.

Observation and charting of the blood pressure not only beforehand, but at frequent and regular intervals during every important or prolonged operation, especially as a guide to the degree of shock, is admitted to be important by all anesthetists.

The anesthetist should give quick warning of any serious fall in the blood pressure, which will enable the surgeon to decide for or against transfusion, for or against attempted extirpation of a brain tumor, for continuing or quickly terminating an operation. This decision can thus be made with scientific accuracy far more surely than by observation of the general physical appearance of the patient. Accurately known blood pressure is of greater value than the rate or quality of the pulse, and as pointed out by Harmer, gives warning from 5 to 20 minutes earlier than the pulse. Moreover, in the doutbful cases it is the most useful.

Prior to operations the anesthetist as well as surgeon should make himself familiar with the condition of the heart, kidneys, blood pressure, hemoglobin, and any unusual condition; should see that the mouth, tongue, teeth and tonsils are in proper condition and that provision be made to prevent chilling of the patient,—an important point never to be overlooked. Chilling and hemorrhage are the most potent factors in producing shock. Chilling by cold solutions and by alcohol used in pre-operative preparations are injurious as demonstrated by *Harmer*.

The anesthetist should provide against certain dangers common to all anesthesias, such as false teeth and other foreign bodies in the mouth, the prevention of paralysis of the musculospiral and other nerves from pressure or from abnormal positions of the arm or leg. I have had one non-fatal case of hemiplegia occurring a few hours after etherization. It is possible but not certain that this was a direct result of the increased blood pressure. Several other similar and sometimes fatal cases have been reported. It is to be remembered that in a few cases a hemiplegia has occurred shortly before the time set for operation. Had the hemiplegia occurred only a few hours or days later it might have occurred during the operation and have been (erroneously) attributed to the ether.

During operation the anesthetist should attend strictly to his own business and especially remember that the first half hour is the period of greatest danger. He should glance at the operation only from time to time, not to study the operation, but in order to anticipate the need for lighter or deeper anesthesia and when the anesthetic may be stopped. Of course he should keep himself constantly informed of the general condition of the patient by observation of the respiration, the most important function of all, of the blood pressure, pulse, pupil, color, and condition of the skin as to sweating.

I believe that an *anesthesia chart* should be kept in every case—even for a brief etherization. How elaborate this should be is a debatable question. The American Surgical Association could do good service, as Lilienthal has suggested in a letter to me, if through a committee it should prepare a standard chart adapted to most hospitals and most anesthetists. I am persuaded that a chart tends to concentrate the attention of the anesthetist upon his "job" and make him more careful. In a few years such charts would also furnish us with very valuable and extensive statistics. The form should be full enough to make it valuable and to compel the average anesthetist to make close and continuous observation, yet not so elaborate and detailed as to defeat its own object. Some especially expert anesthetists would prefer a more elaborate chart for more detailed observations. The American Surgical Association might also prepare this fuller form and each anesthetist could make his choice.

On first seeing the charts used by Boothby[14] I was staggered by their apparent complexity. When analyzed, however, I found there was *less than one observation per minute*. In practice, as I have observed, Boothby easily records them all himself in a quiet leisurely fashion. Instead of distracting attention from the patient, these records fix the anesthetist's attention much more closely upon the patient's condition than if no chart is used. The occasional anesthetist will hardly be able to utilize any but the simplest chart.

If it be objected that a chart, and especially a full one, is a great deal of trouble, I answer:

"Giving ether is a serious business, always attended by possibility of danger. Life may depend on the carefulness of the anesthetist, and this is surely worth any amount of trouble."

One feature of the chart of the Massachusetts General Hospital is exceedingly valuable, viz:—that there is a first or pre-operative part to be filled in by the house officer (surgical or medical), who has had charge of the patient, giving most of the data the anesthetist should know beforehand; a second part relating to the data and conditions during operation to be filled in by the anesthetist; and a third post-operative part to be filled in by the nurse in charge of the case immediately after operation. A *duplicate carbon copy* should be made, the original to be filed with the notes of the case; the copy with the consolidated "Anesthesia Records."

Here the question arises whether a doctor or a woman nurse is in general the more desirable anesthetist. No hard and fast rule can be laid down. Surely no legislative action is called for, though it has been actually proposed. If one has an Alice Magaw (Kessel) or a Florence Henderson of the Mayo Clinic* or a Sister Ethelrida of Murphy's Clinic the decision is easily in favor of the trained nurse. If, however, one has such skilled doctors as we find especially here in Boston and other of our large cities the decision is reversed.

The nurse lives in the hospital and can see the patient at all times. She can soothe the timid patient, who is more often of her own sex, better than most men. She is more vigilant in observing small details. She will be less likely

---

* For two admirable and practical papers see Alice Magaw, Surg., Gynecol. and Obst., 1906, Vol. iii, p. 795, and Collected Papers, Mayo Clinic, 1905-09, p. 567; and Florence Henderson, St. Paul Med. Jour., February, 1914, p 74, and Collected Papers, Mayo Clinic, 1913, p. 701.

to be lured away from the rôle of the professional anesthetist than a man, who too often uses anesthesia merely as a stepping-stone to private surgical practice. A doctor, however, because he has studied medicine, is more thoroughly equipped than a nurse (until her experience runs into hundreds of cases) to appreciate possible or even impending dangers. Moreover, the doctor is less apt to be upset and "flustered" by a sudden perilous emergency. The best solution of all perhaps is an intelligent and alert woman doctor, such as Dr. Isabella C. Herb in Bevan's Clinic. Such Herbs, however, do not grow in every surgical garden.

Personality, intelligence, zeal and quick wit may easily be worth more than greater knowledge.

In order that medical men and women shall devote themselves to anesthesia as a specialty, the public must be taught that safety lies in having an expert anesthetist, and that like any other expert, if he is to obtain a living as such, he must be well paid, otherwise he cannot devote his whole time to this specialty.

I might add also that the profession itself does not yet sufficiently appreciate this same point. Roberts[15] cordially endorses this view. The peril he so valiantly attacked is gradually passing away.

One of the real but infrequent dangers of ether is its *inflammability*. I should probably omit this because of its infrequency had I not had personally what might have been a very serious accident.

Nearly everybody thinks that the vapor from a *volatile* substance of course rises upwards. The etherizer must never forget that the vapor of ether is *heavier* than air and falls downwards. Saturate a bit of gauze with ether. Hold the back of the hand first *above* the gauze and then *below* it and you will never forget that ether vapor falls. In 1863, after Gettysburg, in a large military hospital of 3000 beds in pavilions built wholly of wood, I was trying to secure a large bleeding vessel just above the inner end of the clavicle. The only available light was five candles stuck in five augur holes in a square block of wood and held necessarily very near the ether cone. Suddenly the ether flashed afire, the etherizer flung the glass bottle of ether (it was before the days of our present tin cans) in one direction and the blazing cone fortunately in another. We narrowly escaped a serious conflagration. Why did I not use chloroform, which is non-inflammable, in conditions well known before I began to operate? I fear I must admit gross thoughtlessness. My only consolation is that the patient suffered no harm. Neither he nor I was burned and he recovered without further incident.

So happy an outcome does not always occur, for there are on record a number of cases of more or less serious burns of both patient and surgeon. In one case, when the switch of an electric hand light was turned on to observe the color of the face (the patient being prone) the spark ignited the ether.

"Inflammability of the patient" might also be mentioned as a possible danger to the *surgeon*. Here again I speak from two personal experiences. In one, the patient in his early frenzy, disengaged himself suddenly from the etherizer, scattered the assistants and was about to assault me, when fortunately, a strong Irish orderly who, again fortunately, was standing behind him, so that the dazed patient was not aware of his presence, seized him around the waist and held him till the stage of excitement quickly passed away. Though bound like Samson with many withes, four strong men and the etherizer a few minutes later scarcely prevented his reducing the table to firewood in a second attempt to "get" me.

The other case I relate especially as a warning that no one should *ever* give ether without the presence of another person, except in emergencies when such help *cannot* possibly be obtained.

Many years ago I had to open an abscess in a young man. The etherizer did not appear, and as the patient was suffering I unwisely gave him the ether alone. He had taken only a few inhalations when he was seized with the delusion that I was about to do him harm. With one sweep he threw the ether cone away, leaped up, seized a chair and swinging it high above his head was ready, nay determined, to brain me. As he was an athletic six-footer, and as he stood between myself and the door, fight and flight were equally impossible. I lost no time, you may be sure, in entering what I believe the lawyers call a plea of "confession and avoidance"; a confession of my folly, and a lively avoidance of my enemy. I have always accepted the axiom that two bodies cannot occupy the same space at the same time, but ever since that "episode," as Artemus Ward would have called it, I have been equally convinced that one body *can* be in two places at the same time. The only refuge I did not seek, was under the bed, and the evident reason for my not achieving that ignominious retreat was that my legs would have broken before I could have attained its friendly protection. Don't hint at a "*mauvais quart d'heure.*" Less than two such "bad minutes" more than satisfied me and I am sure would have fully satisfied you.

The incident, which I can now blithely portray as a comedy, thus perhaps making its lesson less quickly forgotten, came perilously near to ending as a tragedy. Had the uplifted chair not been an impediment as well as a weapon, and had I not been forty years younger and forty pounds lighter, you would probably be listening to some other orator today.

In the case of women patients the rule *never* to give ether alone should be *absolute*, for delusional dreams do occasionally occur during anesthesia and are honestly believed after recovery. A charge of assault may easily follow either as a result of this sincere belief, or as a means of blackmail. If no witness was present the only evidence can be the positive assertion by A and the equally positive denial by B. How *can* the most intelligent jury be sure to decide aright? Moreover, if sudden death should occur, a third person as a witness would evidently be most desirable.

Unfortunately I have to confess my own delinquency in not keeping any record of my etherizations. I must, therefore, rely upon my own and my assistants' memories as to any fatalities. Two deaths from chloroform stand out very clearly in my memory, and had I had any from ether I feel quite certain that I should not have forgotten so deplorable an event. I have had several very narrow escapes, but after a most careful review of my cases and conferring with Drs. DaCosta, Taylor and Spencer, who have etherized at least 75% of all my cases, we are all four so fortunate as not to be able to recall a single case of death, either immediate or remote, from ether.

Three of my patients have almost been drowned by an *"inundation of mucus."* One was a boy three or four years old whose mouth, shortly after the operation was begun, looked as if he were blowing soap bubbles. The loud bubbling respiration and his cyanosis could not be misinterpreted. He was saved by the simple expedient of holding him upside down by his heels. Frothy watery mucus poured in a stream from his mouth and nose. In a few moments the operation could be resumed and was completed without further trouble. The second was a man who was similarly rescued by Dr. Taylor's mounting the table, placing the man's legs over his shoulders and thus almost completely inverting him. The third case—a woman—was fortunately in a hospital and on a suitable table. She was at once placed in the extreme Trendelenburg position and quickly relieved. I mention these because I have seen reports of several deaths during operation, which, so far as I could judge, might have been prevented by a similar simple treatment, which is always available.

This "drowning" by mucus, as Connell has pointed out, is most likely to occur in the narrow zone between a light subconscious anesthesia and a profound and asphyxial anesthesia. In that same zone also vomiting and consequent aspiration pneumonia are serious dangers.

The dangers on the cardiac side I need not describe in detail as Dr. Finney[16] considered them fully in 1901 and I have little to add. I may be allowed a moment only to say that I would far rather operate on a case with a bad heart than with bad kidneys. Finney also called attention to the infrequency of deaths from heart disease under ether as compared with their great frequency in the general community. Patients with any cardiac disease of course run greater risks than those with healthy hearts, but as Ochsner has well said, such cases "are safe because they are considered especially unsafe" and therefore extra care is given them.

The chief danger is from myocardial rather than from valvular disease. I may cite a single case as evidence that valvular disease may not be so great a danger as is sometimes believed.

The worst case of valvular disease I have ever seen I operated on in January, 1888,—a woman then 62 years of age with marked tricuspid and mitral regurgitation. I resected the inferior dental nerve for unbearable tic. Ether was very carefully given and no trouble arose. In 1895 at nearly 70 years of age, she required a second operation for a recurrence. Had I not done the first operation myself I might almost have doubted whether the jaw had ever been touched, so perfectly normal did the bone appear and so apparently normal were the nerve and its canal. Her valvular disease had become far worse. Prof. H. A. Hare kindly took charge of the ether. In both operations the Allis inhaler was used. During the second operation the external jugulars were enormously distended and the blood from the wound was very dark, especially toward the end of the operation. Hare writes me: "It was the most serious case of valvular disease that I have seen take an anesthetic. Neither have I ever seen such marked tricuspid regurgitation nor such extraordinary pulsation of the liver in any case, much less one that has been anesthetized. It is interesting to note that the administration of just enough ether to keep her under acted as a stimulant to her heart so that her pulse improved. It was only toward the latter part of the operation that the regurgitation became so great that intense cyanosis developed." Yet she was out of bed on the third day and went home on the sixth. She died two and a half years later. She was a patient of Drs. S. Weir and John K. Mitchell. The latter made the *post mortem* and reported that the right auricle itself was as large as a good sized heart and held the entire fist. The mitral orifice admitted the tips of four fingers, the tricuspid the thumb and three fingers. The pericardial sac was entirely obliterated.

The *respiratory dangers* are even more to be feared than the cardiac. During anesthesia the chief danger is paralysis of the respiratory center; after anesthesia a post-operative pneumonia.

The studies of Haldane, Priestly, Poulton and others in England and of several observers, notably Yandell Henderson of Yale, in this country have brought prominently before the profession the danger of *Acapnia*, i.e. the lack of carbon dioxid.* This gas, formerly regarded only as a noxious waste product, is now believed to be the irritant which calls into activity the extremely sensitive respiratory center.†

Poulton[17] by forced breathing for two and a half minutes before the British Physiological Society, produced such a dangerous acapnia in himself that several of the physiologists ex-

* Henderson has a series of valuable papers in the Amer. Jour. Physiol., 1908-1911, Vols. xxi-xxvii. That on Acapnia and Anesthetics, is in Vol. xxvi, p. 260.

† As noted by Campbell, Douglas, Haldane and Hobson (Jour. Physiology, 1913, Vol. xlvi, p. 301) the facts recently brought forward by Hesselbalch point clearly to the conclusion that what the respiratory center really responds to, when it responds to CO_2, is the balance of H-ion concentration in the blood; and as an increase of 2 m.m. of CO_2 pressure corresponds to a scarcely measurable increase in the H-ion concentration of blood, it follows that the respiratory center is extremely sensitive to changes in the H-ion concentration. (See also Douglas and Haldane, Jour. Physiol., 1909, Vol. xxxviii, p. 420.)

pressed alarm for his life and at least one had to leave the room.

When a patient struggles or screams while being etherized, thus over-ventilating the lungs and dangerously diminishing the carbon dioxid, if the etherizer becomes nervous and gives the ether intermittently, and especially if in these conditions any considerable amount of ether be suddenly poured on the inhaler, it may easily be enough to cause death by reason of its concentration. It must be clearly understood that not the *amount* of ether inhaled, but its *concentration* in the respired air, is the chief danger. Even two or three deep inspirations in such conditions are fraught with danger not only to the respiration but to the heart.[18] Herein lies one of the chief merits of the Connell anesthetometer, as such a sudden concentration is impossible.*

In acapnic cases Henderson suggests a very simple means of temporary re-breathing in order to supply the needed carbon dioxid by holding a (grocer's) paper bag over the mouth and nose for a time. In an emergency the two hands could be placed over the patient's mouth.

It is also possible that not only may there be an insufficiency of the stimulating carbon dioxid but in certain conditions there may be a reduction in the irritability of the respiratory center itself which may add to the danger.† Future experimental research may reveal more clearly these causative conditions and also the means of avoiding them.

"The great hyperpnea produced by a rapid

* The foregoing and some other later statements seem simpler and more easily understood by others than physiologists than if they were in every detail more technically exact.
† See the admirable paper by Peabody, "Studies on Acidosis and Dyspnea in Renal and Cardiac Disease," with references to other papers. Arch. Int. Med., August, 1914, Vol. xiv, p. 236.

fall in the oxygen pressure of the inspired or alveolar air is not due to the direct effect of want of oxygen on the respiratory center, but to that of the carbon dioxid present... in the blood. The action of this carbon dioxid is reinforced by the acid or other products produced by the want of oxygen, so that the threshold pressure at which the carbon dioxid excites the center is lowered.[19]

But besides its effect on the respiratory center, an excessive loss of carbon dioxid, it is claimed,[20] produces paresis of all unstriped muscular fibers, including those of the vascular system. The blood then accumulates in the internal vessels, and so is followed by facial pallor instead of normal pinkness. To guard against this paresis and consequent pallor Bryant and Henderson,[21] who regard acapnia and anoxemia as "the anesthetist's Scylla and Charybdis," propose that his "sailing orders" should be "keep the patient pink." Whether this theory is correct or not, the order is well worth obeying. Under the Equator, however, and in our equatorial fellow citizens I fear that it would hardly be an attainable tint.

In the intestines, it is claimed that this paresis of the unstriped muscle halts peristalsis, thus causing the gas pains which sometimes are a post-operative complaint and may be a serious danger.* But if acapnia is prevented by a preliminary dose of morphin and atropin and by moderate rebreathing during etherization, normal peristalsis, it is claimed, will persist at the end of a laparotomy.

The greatest respiratory danger of ether is *post-operative pneumonia.* While ether itself is,

* Such "gas pains" have not been very common in my own experience and observation.

I believe, a moderate irritant to the air passages (in spite of Rovsing's assertion), undoubtedly the principal cause of such post-operative pneumonia is aspiration of the contents of the mouth. Kelly[22] of Liverpool and Hölscher[23] by putting coloring matters in the mouth have placed the fact of such aspiration beyond doubt. Kelly has shown equally clearly that one of the great advantages of endotracheal insufflation is that this aspiration practically does not occur.

The aspirated matter will consist of the oral mucus (not seldom, be it remembered, laden with the pneumococcus), the discharges from any lingual, oral, dental or tonsillar ulcer or abscess, and the contents of the stomach, which have been vomited but not wholly ejected. Hence the necessity too little appreciated both by surgeons and anesthetists of getting the mouth, tongue, teeth and tonsils in proper condition before operation.†

Besides this, the utmost care should be used by the anesthetist to prevent vomiting if possible. "If on minimal [not, observe, maximal] dosage, the breathing becomes shallow with an occasional deep breath," vomiting is impending. (Connell.) Should it occur, the anesthetist should promote the speedy and complete escape of the vomitus by turning the head sidewise in extension and thus prevent or diminish aspiration. The prevention of aspiration pneumonia lies largely in the hands of the anesthetist. One of my correspondents confesses to having had two deaths on the table from inhalation of the vomitus during recovery from the ether.

But we must not attribute all the pneumonias which follow ether to the irritation of the ether

---

† I have seen foul roots of old teeth which should have been removed some days before the operation extracted by the surgeon at the end of an operation.

itself, to its mode of administration or even to aspiration. Armstrong[24] has shown that pneumonias are especially frequent in cases of septic foci existing at the time of operation and attributes these pneumonias largely to septic emboli, an opinion re-enforced by Beekman[25] of the Mayo Clinic. In operations in the upper abdomen such emboli are especially to be feared. This is due partly to the natural inhibition of diaphragmatic breathing and therefore of full expension of the lower part of the lungs by reason of the pain.

Pneumonias may also follow local anesthesia, in which there can be no question of aspiration. Gottstein[26] and Mikulicz[27] both report larger percentages of pneumonias after local anesthesia than after general anesthesia. The experience in the Mayo Clinic confirms this observation. The probable reason is that the weaker and more serious cases have had local anesthesia. "Most of the lung complications have developed in patients who have been operated on for carcinoma, especially of the stomach, and the autopsy has shown fine metastatic growths in serial sections of the lungs.*"

Anuria fortunately is not a very frequent sequel of ether, but is a very serious one. Ether as a rule decreases the urine for a day or sometimes longer. I always watch the bedside chart with anxiety for the first two or three days to ascertain the urinary output. As a rule after 24 or 48 hours there is a moderate increase. I have lost two patients from anuria. The first was a case of nephro-lithiasis, occurring unfortunately just a year before the discovery of the *x*-rays. I knew of course of the moderate frequency of bilateral renal calculus, and that tem-

* Letter from Miss Henderson.

porary suppression sometimes followed unilateral nephrotomy. In this case during the first 28 hours after the nephro-lithotomy only eleven ounces of urine in all were secreted; in the next four days only twenty-five to twenty-eight ounces daily. In spite of vigorous treatment, the amount fell to fourteen, and then to three and a half ounces with absolute suppression for the last 36 hours. She died on the eighth day. I had anxiously considered the question of an exploratory operation on the other kidney, but there was absolutely no clinical evidence of any stone there. If no stone were found at a second operation and she had died, I should forever have had a burden on my conscience. The x-rays would have decided the question and might have saved her life, for a calculus in the other kidney was found at the *post mortem*.

The other case had a large sarcoma of the shoulder. Removal of the entire half shoulder girdle was the only possible operation. He died in 31 hours, never having secreted a drop of urine.

Chace[28] reports the examination of the urine in 125 consecutive cases. Two cases—with no albuminuria before operation—died from suppression on the seventh day. In the great majority both of normal and abnormal kidneys there is happily only a temporary diminution, but the amount of the urine should always be most carefully recorded and vigilantly watched.

At present it is impossible to predict such suppression. The remedies, such as they are, are well known but may easily be of no avail.

Glycosuria also may follow etherization, as was first shown in dogs by Hawk[29] in 1904. As a rule it is only temporary. Hawk and his associates have shown that this glycosuria, at least in dogs, is especially dependent on diet. A carbohydrate-free diet always was followed by glycosuria while after a mixed diet there was none. That this glycosuria is not wholly the result of etherization (at least in cats) but may be in part an "emotional glycosuria," caused by the excitement attending operation, was first pointed out by Cannon,* and has since been confirmed by others both in this country and in Germany. Henderson and Underhill[30] attribute the glycosuria to acapnia. Higgins and Ogden[31] have shown that injuries of the head were followed by glycosuria in nearly 10% of the cases.

In diabetics it would therefore be advisable to use nitrous oxid and oxygen or, if possible, local anesthesia, since ether might precipitate a fatal diabetic coma.

Acidosis. Recently the dramatic fatal cases reported by Brewer, Beesly and Bevan, and the researches of Crile, Hawk, Bevan and Favill; of your Boston men, Ladd and Osgood, Peabody, Kelly, Brackett Stone and Low, and numerous others, have focussed attention upon acidosis and its various results, especially acetonuria.

Could anything be more distressing than such a case as Brewer's?[32] A boy of 12—a successful operation for appendicitis—everything practically normal till the third night after operation. Then pulse, temperature, and wound all being normal, sudden attacks of terror awaking him from sleep, his screams heard all over the building, increasing somnolence in the intervals, next a sweetish breath, repeated vomiting, acetone and diacetic acid found in the urine and death in 32 hours after the first piercing scream! Such a case breaks a surgeon's heart.

* Proc. Amer. Philosoph. Soc., 1911, p. 227, and Amer. Jour. Physiol., 1911-12, Vol. xxix, p. 261.

The pathological changes in acidosis are especially pronounced in the liver, so much so that Bevan and Favill call it an "hepatic toxemia." Crile† and others have shown that this is a local pathological instance of a more widely distributed normal process. All the activities of the body, every "transformation of energy" produces acid by-products, which in turn must be neutralized if life is to be sustained. The kidney, as pointed out by L. J. Henderson,[33] separates the non-volatile acid from the base of these acid by-products of metabolism, excretes the acids in solution and returns the bases to the blood to be used over again in neutralizing additional acid. The volatile acid—carbon dioxid—escapes by the lungs. The H-ion concentration of the blood (P_H) is an index of the acidity of the blood and of its carbon dioxid[34] content. This carbon dioxid stimulates the respiratory center and also causes an increased output of adrenalin. Crile claims that his histologic and chemical studies have shown that the changes in acidosis are limited to the brain, the adrenals and the liver. Certainly these organs and especially the liver do show marked changes. "While in acidosis the H-ion concentration of the blood is not altered, its *reserve alkalinity* (*i.e.* the ability to retain normal reaction despite the addition of acid) is decreased to a measurable amount."[35] Carbohydrate starvation especially favors acetonuria.

Kelly[36] examined the urine in 400 cases in the Boston City Hospital and found 46 which showed acid intoxication in 17 different disease conditions. Ladd and Osgood[37] in their important paper showed that in 120 patients etherized

† Influence of Inhalation Anesthesia on Acidity of Blood, etc., Annals of Surgery., January, 1915, p. 6; Phenomena of Acidosis, etc., Trans. Amer. Surg. Assn., 1915, both by Crile.

with the Blake cone, acetonuria was found in varying degrees and proportionate to the length of the etherization in 106 (88.5%), whereas in 102 by the open method this percentage fell to 26%, or less than one-third as many as when the cone was employed—a very serious indictment of the cone method. Gatch[25] has emphasized this danger and I think explained the reason for it.

In some cases the symptoms,—persistent vomiting, sweetish (acetone) odor of the breath, peculiarly pink lips, dry tongue and mouth, give us warning. Examination of the blood and urine will convert suspicion into certainty.

The administration of water, glucose and sodium bicarbonate, the lessening of all physical and psychical conditions which increase the transformation of energy are the best preventive remedies. If there is no manifest and speedy improvement no general anesthetic should be given. Local anesthesia should be employed.

But in not a few cases no symptoms whatever betray its approach until the storm bursts in all its fury. Future studies and experiments on animals it is to be hoped may furnish us with warning signals that may enable us to prevent or vanquish this not very common but terrible danger.

What now is the conclusion of the whole matter? In my opinion "straight ether" by the open drop method on an Allis inhaler or a simple mask is by far the best and safest routine anesthetic. I am glad that such staunch upholders of more elaborate and accurately scientific methods of administration, as Boothby and Connell, both uphold this dictum. This is especially the method of choice for doctors who only occasionally give an anesthetic, because the margin of safety with ether is so wide.

In some clinics from which I have replies in exact figures, many thousands of patients have been etherized especially by this method without a death. Alice Magaw (Kessel) and Florence Henderson have to their credit respectively 22,000 and 20,000 administrations without a death. But other clinics have a mortality of one in 5000, one in 3000 to one in 451,* thus bringing the average mortality down to 1 in 7706. Inclusion of the late deaths would make the proportion much less favorable.†

Evidently we ought to and must attain better results, especially when the British surgeons and anesthetists have shown us that they can be realized. To attain these better results we need in my opinion:

1. Many professional anesthetists.
2. The use of an anesthesia chart in all cases.
3. The collection of statistics, best by the American Surgical Association at intervals of five years.
4. Instruction of all medical students in the theory and practice of anesthesia.
5. Straight ether by the open drop method as a routine method instead of mixtures and sequences. I believe all of the latter to be more dangerous than ether.
6. More accurate dosage of the ether by the anesthetometer as a gas on the basis of its anes-

---

* As to this report from one of the ablest of American surgeons, it is but just to state that he only recently began to keep systematic anesthesia records. It is evident from the details he gives that very exceptional cases happened to be operated on during the short period since he began his records. We must all admire his honesty in giving the exact figures.

† All the British and American figures as well as Gurlt's and Rovsing's (see reference No. 5) are to some extent a matter of definition of what is a "death from ether." One surgeon (or anesthetist) would admit and another reject the late pneumonias and alleged "status lymphaticus" (Henderson, Trans. Amer. Surg. Assn., 1911, p. 230), those from intercranial pressure, suppression of urine, etc.

thetic tension, *i.e.* the partial pressure of the ether vapor in the respired air.

Meyer and Gottlieb[39] frankly attribute the great majority of accidents to "faulty management and incautious dosage of the anesthetic" and again (pp. 74-5) to "the administration of too high concentrations of the anesthetic." A knowledge of this concentration or "anesthetic tension" cannot be obtained by observation. It must be by exact measurement in millimeters of mercury.

In spite, therefore, of the splendid results in certain most competent hands, I believe that others less skilled would achieve better results by some such "instrument of precision," and the most skilled and successful would find great comfort in this more exact knowledge.

Science began with the substitution of the balance, the yardstick and the clock, for even the most accurate guesses as to weight, dimension and time. In anesthesia the same I feel *must* hold good.

Of all the apparatuses I am acquainted with, the Connell anesthetometer appeals to me as the best. It deals with ether in the form in which it actually reaches the patient's lungs, that is as a gas and not as a liquid. The tension is easily and quickly regulated according to the needs of the patient. The alcoholic, the child, and the adult all require to be saturated to the same ether tension in order to saturate their tissues up to the point of anesthesia.

Inquiry as to whether any deaths had occurred in cases in which the anesthetometer had been used disclosed only one, a patient at the Brigham Hospital operated on by Dr. Harvey Cushing. Dr. Walter M. Boothby, than whom no one could be more careful or more skilful, gave the anesthetic. The patient was a man with a very large cerebellar tumor pressing upon the medulla. He died from respiratory failure eight minutes after the beginning of the anesthesia. It is very clear, I think, that neither anesthetist, the anesthetic, nor the apparatus was responsible for the fatal result. It was due to the situation and size of the tumor.

I have never seen so smooth an etherization as one by Boothby with the anesthetometer for nearly two hours in one of Cushing's brain cases. The patient's breathing was inaudible throughout, in sharp contrast to the moderately stertorous breathing and coughing of another patient anesthetized elsewhere a few days later by the Roth-Dräger apparatus. The anesthetometer looks complicated, but its management is easily mastered and it then fulfils exactly the requirements just quoted. In fact, I think it is the only apparatus that does. It will be useful only to those who can afford the expense and who are constantly engaged in giving ether, especially in hospitals. It will not supplant the open drop method as a routine method to be used by the great majority. The very accuracy of the apparatus is a temptation to place too implicit reliance upon it, forgetful of the fact that the reaction of the patient and the disease cannot be accurately predicted.

EVERY CASE OF ANESTHESIA IRRESPECTIVE OF THE METHOD EMPLOYED REQUIRES UNREMITTING WATCHFULNESS FROM FIRST TO LAST.

Endotracheal and endopharyngeal insufflation are most valuable additions to our methods.*

* The hybrid Latin and Greek terms "intra-tracheal," "intra-pharyngeal," etc., should be discarded for "endotracheal," "endopharyngeal," etc., derived wholly from Greek. Trachea, pharynx, etc., are not Latin words, but simply Greek terms transferred into Latin as we have transferred menu, chauffeur, etc., into English. Imagine our writing "intra-carditis" or "intra-metrium"!

Thoracic surgery, which for years had lagged behind all other departments of regional surgery, has suddenly broadened and improved by leaps and bounds, as a result first of the differential pressure chambers and later of insufflation methods, so that now all the organs in the chest are freely accessible. One important note of caution sounded by Cotton and Boothby[40] I must repeat and loudly,—there must always be provided a *safety valve* to prevent excessive pressure and serious damage to the lung and the right heart.

What of the future? New anesthetics and improvements in our present methods, possibly even the discovery of the ideal anesthetic, will give us, I hope, a new, a safe and an agreeable anesthetic ere the centenary of anesthesia occurs on October 16, 1946.

Finally: In glorious, yea inspiring, contrast to the work of destruction promoted by other departments of Science, as shown in the present horrible war, is the blessed work of our Guild. In war as in peace, winning victory after victory over disease and death, we devote all our knowledge, skill, and ingenuity, century after century, to the solace and service of Humanity.

REFERENCES.

[1] Prog. Méd., December, 1905, p. 173.
[2] Anesthetics, p. 855.
[3] Gurlt, Arch. klin. Chir., 1897, iv, 473.
[4] Hewitt and Robinson, Anesthetics, London, 1912, p. 139.
[5] Abdominal Surgery, Edited by Pilcher, p. 76. See second footnote, page 29, of this address.
[6] Editorial, Jour. Amer. Med. Assn., April 4, 1914, p. 1098.
[7] Trans. Amer. Surg. Assn., 1915, and Journal American Medical Association, October 23, 1915, p. 1418.
[8] Jour. Amer. Med. Assn., June 11, 1910, p. 1967.
[9] McCullough, Jour. Amer. Med. Assn., Sept. 25, 1915, p. 1090.
[10] Anoci-Association, p. 97.
[11] Prog. Méd., December, 1912, p. 218.
[12] Med. News, March 2, 1895, p. 125.
[13] Annals of Surgery, 1901, Vol. xxxiv, p. 329.
[14] Jour. Pharmacol. and Exp. Therap., March, 1914, p. 329.

[14] The Anesthesia Peril, Therap. Gaz., Feb. 15, 1908.
[15] Trans. Coll. Phys., Phila., 1901, 13.
[17] Johns Hopkins Hosp. Rpts., August, 1910, p. 235.
[18] Henderson, Trans. Amer. Surg. Assn., 1911, p. 234.
[19] Haldane and Poulton, "Effects of Want of Oxygen on Respiration," Jour. Physiol., 1908, Vol. xxvii, p. 390.
[20] Henderson, Amer. Jour. Phys., 1909, Vol. xxiv, p. 66; and Hooker, Amer. Jour. Phys., 1911, Vol. xxiii, p. 361, and Vol. xxxi, p. 47.
[21] Jour. Amer. Med. Assn., July 3, 1915, p. 1.
[22] Brit. Med. Jour., 1912, Vol. ii, p. 17.
[23] Arch. klin. Chir., 1898, Vol. lvii, p. 175.
[24] Brit. Med. Jour., May 19, 1906, p. 1141.
[25] Annals of Surgery, 1913, Vol. lvii, p. 718.
[26] Arch. klin. Chir., 1898, Vol. lvii, p. 409.
[27] Verhandl. Deutsch. Gesellsch. Chir., 1901, Part ii, p. 560.
[28] Postgraduate, N. Y., 1904, Vol. xix, p. 302.
[29] Arch. Int. Med., July, 1911, Vol. viii, p. 39.
[30] Amer. Jour. Physiol., 1911, Vol. xxviii, p. 275.
[31] Boston Med. and Surg. Jour., Feb. 21, 1895, p. 197.
[32] Annals of Surgery, 1902, Vol. xxxvi, p. 481.
[33] Jour. Biol. Chem., 1911, Vol. ix, p. 408.
[34] Peabody: "Studies on Acidosis and Dyspnea in Renal and Cardiac Disease," Arch. Int. Med., August, 1914, Vol. xiv, p. 236.
[35] Van Slyke, Stillman and Cullen, Proc. Soc. Exp. Med. and Biol., 1914-1915, Vol. xii, p. 165.
[36] Annals of Surg., 1905, Vol. xli, p. 161.
[37] Annals of Surgery, 1907, Vol. xlvi, p. 460.
Since the delivery of this address an interesting statistical paper on the "Examination of the Urine in 214 Consecutive Cases in Deaver's Clinic" by Bradner and Reismann has been published in the American Journal of Medical Science, Nov., 1915, p. 727.
[38] Trans. Amer. Surg. Assn., 1911, p. 198.
[39] Pharmacol. Clinical and Exp., Translated by Hasley, Lippincott, 1914, p. 68.
[40] Boston Med. and Surg. Jour., March 28, 1912, p. 486.

Printed by Libri Plureos GmbH in Hamburg, Germany